Contents

Introduction
What this book contains   3
How to set, mark and interpret the tests   3
Helping your child sit tests   4
What to do with the results   5

English
Testing your child's English   6
Reading tests   8
Writing tests   21
Spelling and handwriting test   24
Answers   26

Mathematics
Testing your child's mathematics   35
Test 1 (Level 3)   36
Test 2 (Level 4)   40
Test 3 (Level 5)   45
Answers   50

Science
Testing your child's science   52
Science test   53
Answers   63

Text © ST(P), Wendy and David Clemson, Sean McArdle and Wendy Wren 1996

The right of ST(P), Wendy and David Clemson, Sean McArdle and Wendy Wren to be identified as the authors of this work has been asserted by them in accordance with the Copyright, Designs and Patents Act 1988.

All rights reserved. The copyright holders authorise ONLY users of *Practice Papers for the Key Stage 2 National Tests* to make photocopies or stencil duplicates of page 32 for their own immediate use. No other rights are granted without permission in writing from the publishers or under licence from the Copyright Licensing Agency Limited. Further details of such licences (for reprographic reproduction) may be obtained from the Copyright Licensing Agency Limited of 90 Tottenham Court Road, London W1P 9HE. Copy by any other means or for any other purpose is strictly prohibited without prior written consent from the copyright holders. Application for such permission should be addressed to the publishers.

Acknowledgements
The publishers wish to thank the following for permission to use copyright material:

Peters Fraser & Dunlop Group Ltd on behalf of the author for an extract from *Cry of the Seagulls* by Monica Dickens, HarperCollins Publishers, 1986; G.M. Wilson for 'Old Johnny Armstrong' by Raymond Wilson.

Every effort has been made to trace all the copyright holders but if any have been inadvertently overlooked the publishers will be pleased to make the necessary arrangement at the first opportunity.

First published in 1996 by
Stanley Thornes (Publishers) Ltd
Ellenborough House
Wellington Street
CHELTENHAM GL50 1YW

96 97 98 99 00 / 10 9 8 7 6 5 4 3 2

A catalogue record for this book is available from the British Library.

ISBN 0 7487 2763 9

Introduction

What this book contains

During your child's last year in primary school (Year 6) he or she will sit Key Stage 2 National Assessment Tests in the three core subjects: English, mathematics and science. These tests take place in school over a period of about a week during May and the results are reported back to you and are also passed on to the secondary school your child will attend. For each of the three subjects your child will be given a mark in the form of a level. Most children will perform in the range of Levels 3–5 by the end of Key Stage 2 with an average performance being roughly Level 4.

The tests are a valuable measure of your child's performance in school. Not only will they be influential in the secondary school's initial assessment, they may also be your child's first experience of sitting formal written tests. It is extremely helpful if that first experience can be a positive one.

This book provides you with one complete set of practice papers for each of the three subjects with the principle aim of preparing your child confidently for the tests. Each set of papers will:

- provide test questions similar to those in the National Tests for Levels 3–5 of the National Curriculum.

- give your child practice in sitting the tests: working to a set time, getting familiar with the format and style of the tests and developing effective test strategies.

- give you a broad guide to your child's likely level of performance within Levels 3–5 of each subject.

- give you an idea of strengths and weaknesses in your child's learning.

How to set, mark and interpret the tests

The tests for the three subjects require different lengths of time to complete. The shortest is science (30 minutes); English and mathematics each have up to three papers which require about $2\frac{1}{4}$ hours. In school such papers will be set over a period of about a week. At home, in order to keep the process relaxed, you will probably want to spread the papers over a longer period.

Each set of papers allows you to set, mark and level your child's work in the subjects without any prior knowledge of the National Curriculum. First read the detailed advice on setting the papers; then set the test. When your child has finished each paper use the answers to mark it. Enter the number of marks gained on the papers as shown on the next page.

Add up the marks on each page and enter them at the foot of the page. Add the marks for all the pages to find the total mark obtained, then use the conversion box at the end of the answers to get an idea of National Curriculum level.

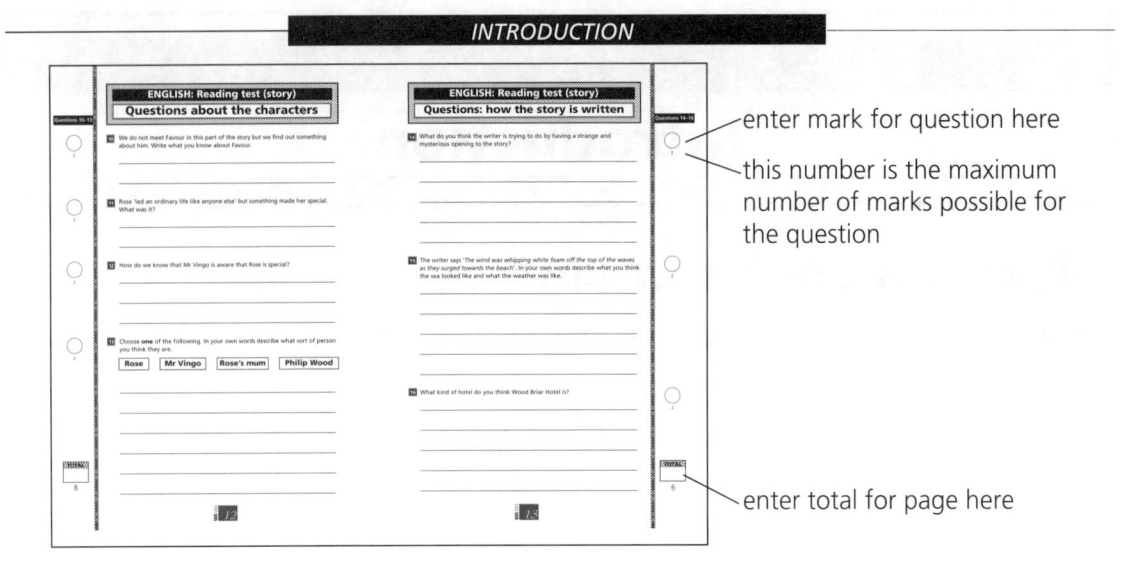

Helping your child sit tests

As well as practising the content of the tests, one of the key aims of this book is to give your child practice in working under test conditions. All the tests are timed and your child should try to complete each one within the given time. In order to make best use of the tests, and to ensure that the experience is a positive one for your child, it is helpful to follow a few basic principles:

- Talk with your child first before embarking on the tests. Present the activity positively and reassuringly. Encourage your child to view doing the papers as an enjoyable activity which will help, always making him or her feel secure about the process.

- Ensure that your child is relaxed and rested before doing a test. It may be better to do a paper at the weekend or during the holidays rather than straight after a day at school.

- Ensure a quiet place, free from noise or disturbance, for doing the tests.

- Ensure that there is a watch or clock available.

- Ensure that your child understands exactly what to do for each paper and give some basic test strategies for tackling the task. For example:

  - Try to tackle all the questions but don't worry if you can't do some. Put a pencil mark by any you can't do, leave them and come back at the end.

  - Make sure you read the questions carefully.

  - Go straight on to the next page when each is finished.

  - Try to pace yourself over the allowed time. Look over the whole paper first to get an idea of how many questions there are. Don't spend too long over one question.

  - Use all your time.

  - If you have any time over at the end go back over your answers. This is particularly important if you are doing one big piece of work, such as writing a story.

INTRODUCTION

- Taking the time to talk over a test beforehand and to discuss any difficulties afterwards will really help your child to gain confidence in the business of sitting tests.

- However your child does, ensure that you give plenty of praise for effort.

What to do with the results

The tests in this book and the results gained from them are only a guide to your child's likely level of performance. They are not an absolute guarantee of how your child will actually perform in the National Tests themselves. However, these papers will at least allow your child to get practice in sitting tests; they will also give *you* an insight into the strengths and weaknesses in their learning.

If there are particular areas of performance which seem weaker, it may be worth providing more practice of the skills required. It is also valuable to discuss any such weaknesses with your child's class teacher, and to seek confirmation of any problem areas and advice on how to proceed. It is always better to work in partnership with the school if you can. Above all ensure that you discuss these issues with your child in a positive and supportive way so that you have their co-operation in working together to improve learning.

ENGLISH
Testing your child's English

What do the National Tests cover?

At Key Stage 2 your child will be studying three areas of English in school. These are:

1. Speaking and Listening
2. Reading
3. Writing

The national tests cover only reading and writing and set three papers for Levels 3–5: Reading; Writing; Spelling and Handwriting.

We have provided papers for each of these three tests. You will find that the tests for English are slightly more intricate than those for the other subjects and each one is different in style. Instructions for setting each one are detailed below. After the tests have been done, you will have to add together the marks from each paper to gain an impression of your child's overall performance in English. This is explained in the Answers section on page 34.

Setting the reading test (time: 60 minutes)

1. The reading test involves reading and answering questions on:
   - a story
   - a poem
   - a piece of informational writing

   The aim of the assignment is to test children's ability to read, understand and respond to different types of writing. The national test does this as one paper and allows one hour for it. You can either set it as a complete paper or do each part separately. We suggest for ease of practice that you break the reading test into three short tests.

2. Set the story reading paper as follows:
   - You will find the story on pages 8–10. Allow your child ten minutes to read it through. Encourage them to read it carefully and more than once if there is time.
   - Your child now has to answer the twenty questions about the story on pages 10–14. Allow 20 minutes for this. The story can be referred back to whilst answering the questions. It may be helpful to jot notes on the story or to underline useful information. Before answering the questions ensure that the procedure is understood.
   - Questions 1 to 8 require one right answer to be ringed.
   - Question 9 requires ordering events in the story by numbering.
   - The remaining questions require written answers. Some require only one- or two-word answers, others will be more lengthy. This is not a test of spelling, punctuation or grammar but children should be as accurate as possible when answering.
   - Any questions which seem difficult to answer should be left and returned to at the end if time allows.

3. Set the poetry paper in a similar way:
   - Allow five minutes to read the poem on page 15 through carefully.
   - Allow ten minutes to answer the questions on pages 16 and 17. Refer back to the poem and jot notes around it if helpful.
   - Remind your child to answer as many as possible. Leave any questions that seem too difficult and come back to them at the end.

4. Set the information paper in a similar way:
   - Allow five minutes to read the piece on page 18 through carefully.
   - Allow ten minutes to answer the questions on pages 19 and 20. Refer back to the passage and jot notes around it if helpful.
   - Remind your child to leave and come back to any difficult questions.

Setting the writing test (time: 60 minutes)

1. The writing test involves writing either a story or a piece of non-narrative writing, such as a description or a letter. This book provides the option of writing a story or a letter. Talk to your child about which he or she would like to do. Explain that spelling, grammar and punctuation are important in this piece of work. Allow one hour for the test whichever option is chosen.

2. If your child wishes to write a letter for the test, proceed as follows:
   - The child will need to use the planning sheet on page 21 and the letter starting point on the top of page 23. Paper to write the letter on will also be required.
   - Start by explaining that you will read aloud the letter starting point and proceed to do so.
   - Now introduce the planning sheet and talk through with your child the various

headings. Your discussion should focus on the key features of a letter:

- The importance of being aware of the subject of the letter and the reason for writing it.
- The need to have a good opening to get the reader's attention.
- The need to keep the reader's attention throughout the piece of writing.
- The need to end in an appropriate way.
- The layout of letters and the right style for the reader. Remind your child that you use different tones to write to a bank and to write to a friend.

- Now tell your child that they have 15 minutes to make notes for the letter on the planning sheet. Remember that notes can be very short, maybe just a few words, to get the main ideas down.
- After 15 minutes it is time to write the letter. Give a short break if required. Forty-five minutes is given for writing the letter, using the planning sheet as a structure.
- Remind your child of the time and let them know when there are 15 minutes left. If the work is finished early encourage your child to reread it carefully, checking grammar, punctuation and spelling.

3 If your child wishes to write a story proceed as follows:

- They will need to use the planning sheet on page 22 and the story starting sheet at the bottom of page 23. Paper to write the story on will also be required.
- Start by explaining that there is a choice of two story starting points but that only one should be chosen. Read them both aloud and ask your child to choose one.
- Now introduce the planning sheet and talk through with your child the various headings. Your discussion should focus on the key features of a story:
  - the importance of establishing the setting and the plot of the story as quickly as possible;
  - the need to keep the number of characters manageable so that there is time to describe them adequately and make the reader feel that they know the characters through what they do and say;
  - the importance of a good strong opening to get the reader interested;
  - the need to continue the story in such a way that the reader 'needs to know' what is going to happen;
  - the importance of ending the story well and not leaving it hanging in mid air.

- Remind your child that this has to be a complete short story, and not an episode from a longer one.
- Now tell your child that they have 15 minutes to make notes for the story on the planning sheet. Remember that only one story starter can be chosen and its title should be written at the top. Remember that ideas can be in note form to save time.
- After 15 minutes it is time to write the story. Give a short break if required. Forty-five minutes is available for writing the story and the planning sheet should be used as a structure.
- Remind your child of the time and let them know when there is 15 minutes left. If the work is finished early encourage careful re-reading to check grammar, punctuation and spelling.

Setting the spelling and handwriting test (time: 15 minutes)

1 The spelling test

The spelling test is a short passage with words missed out that your child has to spell. Proceed as follows:

- Turn to page 24 and show your child the passage with the words missed out. On page 32 you will find a complete copy of the passage. You will need either to cut this out or to photocopy it.
- Read the complete passage aloud clearly while your child follows the incomplete one without writing anything.
- Explain that you are going to read the passage again slowly, whilst your child writes in the missing words as clearly as possible.
- Tell your child that if they are unsure of a spelling they should put the letters which they think are right.
- Now read the passage again slowly, pointing out the missing words and giving time to write the word on the appropriate line.
- Allow ten minutes for the whole test.

2 The handwriting test

- The handwriting test on page 25 is a short passage which follows on from the spelling test.
- Read your child the instructions which appear on the sheet above the passage to be copied.
- Allow five minutes for the handwriting test.

ENGLISH: Reading test (story)
The Cry of the Seagull

Something was going to happen. Rose felt restless, charged with an electric feeling of excitement.

Needing to be out of doors, she ran out of the Wood Briar Hotel, crossed the road and climbed the soft sand of the dunes until she could see the sea. The wind was whipping white foam off the top of the waves as they surged towards the beach. What was there for her in the wind? Was Favour somewhere out there, the legendary grey horse of history, who came back to earth again and again as a power for good?

When she became thirteen, Rose Wood had been chosen as one of the special messengers in his crusade against evil and cruelty. Although she led an ordinary life like anyone else, at any moment the mysterious horse might call her, challenging her to the next adventure.

With her short straight hair blown back, she listened and stared so hard that her eyeballs hurt. Nothing. The wind and the sea and the hurrying clouds had no message for her yet. Soon, but not yet. The electric excitement died. She was ordinary Rose again.

As she came through a gap in the dunes on to the road, she saw the ponderous bulk of Mr Vingo plodding along at the edge of the sand.

Rose ran to meet him. 'I'm glad you're back.' Mr Vingo lived at the Wood Briar Hotel, but when he returned after one of his mysterious disappearances, Rose knew enough not to ask, 'Where have you been?'

She took his bag and slung it over her shoulder.

'What's noo?' Mr Vingo had picked that up from Rose's American friend Abigail.

'Nothing exactly. But something's going to happen soon. I know it.' She looked up at his broad, creased face to see if he knew anything.

'Good.' When he smiled, the features of his loose-skinned face rearranged themselves into a different landscape. 'Are you ready, Rose of all Roses?'

'I hope so.' The excitement began to build in her again, a thrilling premonition that started at her fingers and toes and surged into the pit of her stomach.

Opposite the hotel, they waited for a few cars to pass them. A motorcycle was coming, but Mr Vingo stepped into the road without looking, and instead of avoiding him, the faceless rider in white helmet and studded black leather jacket swerved towards him and might have hit him if Rose hadn't pulled him roughly back.

Mr Vingo sat heavily down in the sand. Rose shrieked after the motorcycle. The man...boy...woman – you couldn't tell – did not look around, but on the back of its white helmet a huge glaring eye menaced her, and was gone in a cloud of sand blown off the dunes.

She pulled Mr Vingo up and they crossed the road and went round the corner to the side door that led up to his turret room over the corner verandah.

'Look out!'

Something large and bulky fell out of the sky, missing their heads by inches. A vinyl suitcase. Rose looked up to see where it had come from and saw her father on the roof, hurling a smaller suitcase savagely down on to the gravel path. He was doing his job as a quality tester of new products, to see if 'Lifetime Luggage' was really indestructible.

'Obviously –' Mr Vingo was out of breath '– a day for almost getting killed.' He raised his hat to where Philip Wood stood on a flat part of the roof between two gables, a duffel bag in his arms, his thinning hair wild in the wind.

'Good day to you, sir!' Mr Vingo called up politely.

'Good day to you!' Rose's father chucked down the duffel bag.

Inside the hotel, the twin Miss Mumfords grabbed Rose in the hall.

'Call the police!' Miss Angela's head shook more than ever. 'There's a madman on the roof.'

'My sister saw him,' Miss Audrey held on to Rose's arm in a tight pinch. 'Trying to kill us all.'

'It's only my father.' Rose shook her arm free. She wanted to go through to the kitchen, but they blocked her way, side by side like Tweedledum and Tweedledee with short legs and square overcoats and green woollen berets at the same severe angle.

'Not fit to run a hotel,' Miss Audrey's head shook too.

'He doesn't run it. My mother does.'

'After a fashion,' Miss Audrey said rudely. 'We're packing our bags and leaving.'

'Let me know when you want me to carry them down.' Rose dodged past them.

The elderly Miss Mumfords were always threatening to leave, but they never did.

ENGLISH: Reading test (story)

They stayed all winter, complaining, left in May and were back at the end of September as faithfully as the sea fog, and as boring.

Professor Henry Watson, retired from the University, had been here all winter too. He had come for a week's rest after pneumonia and stayed on because he liked the friendliness of this small hotel and Rose's mother Mollie played backgammon with him and understood his special diet. A retired couple had been staying for the last three weeks while their house was being decorated. Couples and single people and travelling foreigners came for a few days, and various salesmen stayed for a night or two while they were doing business in the nearby town of Newcome. Rose's friend Ben Kelly and his family might come for Easter, but there had been no word. Perhaps. Perhaps not.

When she fed her hamster in his cage in her room, she told him, 'Ben's coming,' as a good luck prophecy, and before she went to bed she washed her hair and cut her straggly fringe.

From *The Cry of the Seagull* by Monica Dickens

ENGLISH: Reading test (story)
Questions about the story

Questions 1–9

Draw a ring around the right answer.

1 At the beginning of the story Rose feels

| bored | that something is going to happen | frightened | upset |

2 Favour was

| an hotel | a special messenger | a horse | a cat |

3 Mr Vingo lived

| at the hotel | on the beach | on a boat | in a flat |

4 Abigail was

| Mr Vingo's friend | Rose's friend | Favour's friend | Miss Angela's friend |

4

ENGLISH: Reading test (story)

5 Mr Vingo was almost run over by

| a car | a truck | a motor cycle | a bus |

6 Something large and bulky fell out of the sky. It was

| a motorcycle | Mr Vingo's bag | a white helmet | a suitcase |

7 Miss Angela and Miss Audrey were

| mother and daughter | twins | friends | cousins |

8 Who ran the Wood Briar Hotel?

| Miss Angela Mumford | Mr Philip Wood | Mr Vingo | Rose's mother |

9 Here are some things which happen in the story. Put them in the right order by numbering each line. The first one has been numbered for you.

_____ Rose saw Mr Vingo coming along the edge of the sand.

_____ Rose fed her hamster and washed her hair.

_____ Outside the hotel Mr Vingo was nearly knocked over.

1 Rose ran out of the hotel and on to the sand.

_____ The Miss Mumfords complained to Rose about her father.

_____ Rose carried Mr Vingo's bag back to the hotel.

_____ Rose and Mr Vingo were nearly hit by a suitcase.

ENGLISH: Reading test (story)
Questions about the characters

10 We do not meet Favour in this part of the story but we find out something about him. Write what you know about Favour.

_____

_____

11 Rose 'led an ordinary life like anyone else' but something made her special. What was it?

_____

_____

12 How do we know that Mr Vingo is aware that Rose is special?

_____

_____

_____

13 Choose **one** of the following. In your own words describe what sort of person you think they are.

| Rose | Mr Vingo | Rose's mum | Philip Wood |

_____

_____

_____

_____

_____

TOTAL 8

ENGLISH: Reading test (story)
Questions: how the story is written

Questions 14–16

14 What do you think the writer is trying to do by having a strange and mysterious opening to the story?

_____

_____

_____

_____

_____

2

15 The writer says *'The wind was whipping white foam off the top of the waves as they surged towards the beach'*. In your own words describe what you think the sea looked like and what the weather was like.

_____

_____

_____

_____

_____

2

16 What kind of hotel do you think Wood Briar Hotel is?

_____

_____

_____

_____

2

TOTAL

6

ENGLISH: Reading test (story)
Questions: your opinion

Questions 17–20

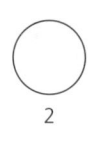

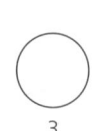

17 Did you enjoy reading the beginning of this story?

    Yes _____   No _____

Explain, giving your reasons, if you would like to read the rest of the story or not.

_____

_____

_____

3

18 Rose was sure something was going to happen. What do you think was going to happen?

_____

_____

_____

3

19 Write about the part of the story you found amusing.

_____

_____

_____

2

20 Would you like to live at Wood Briar Hotel?

    Yes _____   No _____

Explain your reasons using parts of the story to help you.

_____

_____

_____

3

TOTAL 11

OVERALL SCORE 40

ENGLISH: Reading test (poetry)
Old Johnny Armstrong

Old Johnny Armstrong's eighty or more
    And he humps like a question mark
Over two gnarled sticks he shuffles and picks
    His slow way to Benwell Park.

He's lived in Benwell his whole life long
    And remembers how street-lights came,
And how once on a time they laid a tram-line,
    Then years later dug up the same!

Now he's got to take a lift to his flat,
    Up where the tall winds blow
Round a Council Block that rears like a rock
    From seas of swirled traffic below.

Old Johnny Armstrong lives out his life
    In his cell on the seventeenth floor,
And it's seldom a neighbour will do him a favour
    Or anyone knock on his door.

With his poor hands knotted with rheumatism
    And his poor back doubled in pain,
Why, day after day, should he pick his slow way
    To Benwell Park yet again?–

O the wind in park trees is the self-same wind
    That first blew on a village child
When life freshly unfurled in a green, lost world
    And his straight limbs ran wild.

Raymond Wilson

ENGLISH: Reading test (poetry)
Questions

1 What details from the poem show you that Johnny Armstrong has lived in Benwell a long time?

2 Explain, in your own words, the meaning of:

   a. 'he humps like a question mark'

   b. 'his cell on the seventeenth floor'

3 How do you think the poet wants you to feel about the old man?

ENGLISH: *Reading test (poetry)*

4 Why do you think that Johnny Armstrong goes to Benwell Park 'day after day'?

5 What sort of people do you think his neighbours are?

6 Who do you think the village child is in the last verse of the poem?

ENGLISH: Reading test (information)
Children in Elizabethan times

In Elizabethan times, children were thought of as 'small adults'. This being the case, they had to become useful as soon as possible. It was generally accepted that children should help their parents to earn a living from a very early age.

Poor children who were looked after by the parish were sent to live with foster mothers who taught them some craft at which they could earn a few pennies. Older children had to learn a trade. They lived with a 'master' who was responsible for teaching them their trade, giving them somewhere to live and feeding them. While they were learning they were not paid.

How these children were treated depended very much on what the master was like. He might be cruel and heartless or he might be kind and understanding. In general, however, the system worked well. The young person was usually regarded as part of the family and not looked upon as cheap labour.

Many children worked in the cloth industry at this time. Most spinning was done at home and kept very young children 'employed'. Farming was another area where children worked. Bird-scaring was done by children as soon as they could toddle. Clearing stones from land, sheep shearing, loading carts and winnowing were also things in which children became skilled at a very early age.

ENGLISH: Reading test (information)

Questions

1 Why was it accepted in Elizabethan times that children should work from a very early age?

2

2 Why do you think some children had to be 'looked after by the parish'?

2

3 What happened to the children who were 'looked after by the parish'?

2

4 How did older children learn a trade?

3

TOTAL

9

ENGLISH: Reading test (information)

5 How were the children who lived with a 'master' usually regarded?

6 In which two types of work were children often employed?

7 Give three examples of tasks children were expected to do on a farm.

8 In your opinion, should children have been made to work at such an early age? Give reasons for your answer.

ENGLISH: Writing test
Letter planning sheet

How will you begin your letter if:

you know the person's name

_____

you do not know the person's name

_____

Are you writing the letter because:

you want to complain (what about?)

_____

you want information (what about?)

_____

you are pleased about something (what?)

_____

Make notes on what you will write in your letter.

_____

_____

_____

_____

How will you end your letter if:

you know the person's name

_____

you do not know the person's name

_____

ENGLISH: Writing test

Story planning sheet

Title
_____

Setting

where does your story take place?
_____

when does it happen?
_____

Characters

who are they?
_____

what do they look like?
_____

what sort of people/animals are they?
_____

Opening

how will you begin your story?
_____

Middle

what happens in your story?
_____

End

how will you finish your story?
_____

ENGLISH: Writing test
Letter starting point

Where to go, what to see?

A friend who lives in another country is coming to your area for a holiday.

Write a letter to give your friend information about things to see and do on holiday, and places to avoid! You do not have to write about things which are actually in your area. You can make up exciting places and events if you want to.

OVERALL SCORE

20

ENGLISH: Writing test
Story starting point

1 Choose **one** of these starting points for your story.

Write a short story with the title *'The Haunted House'*.

2 Write a short story which opens with the sentence *'The fox crept under the fence and into the garden'*.

OVERALL SCORE

20

ENGLISH: Spelling and handwriting test
Trapped!

1 James was very _____. He had no idea _____ his parents were taking him on _____. His mother said it was going to be a _____. It had been _____ when he had woken up but now the sun was shining.

Suddenly, he _____ that he hadn't packed his football so he rushed out of the _____ and into the shed. There it was, in the _____ , almost hidden _____ a _____ of old _____. As he _____ down to pick it up there was a loud _____ . The shed door had _____ shut! There were no windows in the shed and he was in total _____.

_____ , his eyes _____ as there was _____ light coming through a crack in the door for him to see a little. _____ he _____ his way to the door, tripping over _____ rags and bits of _____. An _____ brushed his face and he let out a loud _____. At last he felt the door _____ but _____ by _____ nor pulling could he get it open. He began to _____ the _____ and shout loudly in the hope that _____ would hear him.

ENGLISH: Spelling and handwriting test

Here is a short passage that finishes the story. Write it out below very neatly in your own handwriting. Remember to make your writing as neat as possible, joining your letters if you can.

2 James's father was passing by the shed at that moment and heard the shouting and rattling. He opened the door and was amazed to see James come tumbling out, blinking in the bright sunlight.

OVERALL SCORE

ENGLISH ANSWERS
Reading tests

To gain an impression of your child's overall performance in English you will have to add together the marks from each paper. You will find this explained in detail on page 34.

Story

1	Rose feels that something is going to happen	*1 mark*
2	Favour was a horse.	*1 mark*
3	Mr Vingo lived at the hotel.	*1 mark*
4	Abigail was Rose's friend.	*1 mark*
5	Mr Vingo was almost run over by a motor cycle.	*1 mark*
6	It was a suitcase.	*1 mark*
7	Miss Angela and Miss Audrey were twins.	*1 mark*
8	Rose's mother	*1 mark*

9
1. Rose ran out of the hotel and on to the sand.
2. Rose saw Mr Vingo coming along the edge of the sand.
3. Rose carried Mr Vingo's bag back to the hotel.
4. Outside the hotel Mr Vingo was nearly knocked over.
5. Rose and Mr Vingo were nearly hit by a suitcase.
6. The Miss Mumfords complained to Rose about her father.
7. Rose fed her hamster and washed her hair. *7 marks*

10 Favour was a 'legendary grey horse who came back to earth again and again as a power for good.' *2 marks*

11 Rose was special because she had been chosen by Favour 'as one of his special messengers in his crusade against evil and cruelty'. *2 marks*

12 When Rose tells Mr Vingo that something's going to happen soon he is not surprised but asks her if she is ready. *2 marks*

13 **Rose:** special (Favour has chosen her); kind (carried Mr Vingo's bag); brave (pulled Mr Vingo out of the way of the motor cycle).
Mr Vingo: gets on well with children; vague (doesn't look when he steps into the road); has a sense of humour (says 'Obviously a day for almost getting killed' when the suitcase nearly hits him); polite.
Rose's mum: runs the hotel; has time for people (Professor Watson).
Philip Wood: seems quite an odd character (throwing suitcases off the roof). *2 marks*

14 Create a mysterious atmosphere; keep the reader guessing so they will read on; immediately capture the reader's attention. *2 marks*

15 The sea was rough and moving swiftly. It was windy and the wind was strong enough to cause the waves to foam. *2 marks*

16 Small, pleasant family hotel where most people feel comfortable and 'at home'. *2 marks*

17 Award no marks for just 'Yes' or 'No'. Award up to 3 marks for reasons given. *3 marks*

ENGLISH: Answers

18 Award up to 3 marks for explanation given which should reflect what the reader already knows about Favour and Rose. *3 marks*

19 Award up to 2 marks for picking out either the exchange with the Miss Mumfords or the behaviour of Mr Wood. *2 marks*

20 Award up to 3 marks for explanations which reflect what the reader knows about the hotel. *3 marks*

Poetry

1 He remembers when street lights came to Benwell/when tram lines where laid/when the tram lines were dug up. *3 marks*

2 a. He is bent over with age and looks like the shape of a question mark. *2 marks*
b. He lives in a high rise building on the 17th floor and his room is as bare and comfortless as a prison cell. *2 marks*

3 The poet wants the reader to feel sorry for the old man. *2 marks*

4 Something to do/for company/to get out of his flat.
Award 2 marks for any of these reasons. *2 marks*

5 Unkind/uncaring/keep themselves to themselves
Award 1 mark for any of these reasons. *1 mark*

6 The village child is the old man in his youth. *3 marks*

Information

1 Children were regarded as 'small adults' so it was thought that they should be useful. *2 marks*

2 They were either orphans or their parents were too poor to look after them. *2 marks*

3 They were sent to live with foster mothers and taught a craft. *2 marks*

4 They lived with a 'master'. (*1 mark*)
He taught them a trade. (*1 mark*)
They were fed and housed. (*1 mark*) *3 marks*

5 This depended on the master but they were usually treated as one of the family. *2 marks*

6 The cloth industry and farming *2 marks*

7 Any 3 of the following: bird scaring/clearing stones from land/sheep shearing/loading carts/winnowing. *3 marks*

8 Award no marks for an opinion with no reasons. Award up to 3 marks for a considered answer which refers to evidence in the passage and a further mark for an original point. *4 marks*

ENGLISH ANSWERS
Writing tests

In order to get an idea of your child's level in writing you will need to assess the writing under three headings:

1. Purpose and organisation
2. Grammar
3. Styles

Children do not develop at the same rate across these three areas so dividing up the marks in this way allows you to see your child's strengths and weaknesses. Marking writing requires you to make judgements about the quality of the writing rather than just ticking right and wrong answers. Guidance for deciding your child's level performance against the three headings is given below. Once you have decided which level description best fits your child's work for each heading award the number of marks shown for that level. Add together the marks they have gained under each heading to get an overall score for writing.

Story writing

Purpose and organisation

What you are looking at under this heading is the content of the story.

Level 2

Look for:

- A clear opening to the story. Your child may use story language such as 'One day', 'Once upon a time', 'It was Sunday and ...'.

- Two or more events in sequence. At this level the events will be little more than a list of what happens. They will not be described in detail.

- Character(s) will be introduced. Your child will probably only give the name of the character(s) and you will not feel you know either what they look like or their personality.

Marking: 4 marks

Level 3

Look for:

- A simple but appropriate ending. This gives evidence that your child has thought through where the story is going. Inappropriate endings which often occur include 'And then I woke up', 'And then I died'!

- A setting for the story. Your child will begin to give details of where the story takes place. Some description such as 'It was dark in the wood ...', 'The snow covered the trees ...'.

- More detailed description of character. This includes a physical description of the character(s) such as 'Jane was tall and had red hair ...'. Also how the character(s) might be feeling, 'He was sad because he had lost his football ...'.

- How will the reader react? Your child will have some idea of what they want their story to 'feel' like. As the reader are you amused, frightened, unhappy?

Marking: 6 marks

ENGLISH: Answers

Level 4

Look for:

- Paragraphs. Your child will have used paragraph divisions to separate the beginning and/or ending from the rest of the story. The correct form of paragraphing is by indenting on a new line, but simply beginning a new line or missing a line is acceptable at this level.

- Events are logically related. The events of the story will be more detailed and should follow on from one another logically. Your child will not have assumed that you know something has happened.

- Beginning, middle and end. As a reader you will begin to get the feeling that the story has a beginning, middle and end. It is not rambling and inconclusive.

- Interaction between characters. The characters in the story should relate to one another. If one character is hurt, another character should react appropriately, e.g. showing concern. If one character tells a joke, another character may laugh or say 'I've heard that one before'.

- Developing character. As the reader you should begin to feel you are getting to know the characters through what your child tells you about them, through what they say or through what other characters say about them.

Marking: 8 marks

Level 5

Look for:

- Paragraphs. Your child should be using paragraphs in the body of the story for such things as a new event, a change of scene, introduction of a new character etc.

- Events. Your child may attempt to introduce a second set of events such as a flashback where the writer or one of the characters relates events that have happened earlier which have a bearing on the story.

- Beginning. The opening of the story will be convincing and your child may have experimented by starting with dialogue, or by having a mysterious opening, the details of which are revealed as the story progresses.

- Middle. The body of the story will have elements of dialogue, action and description.

- End. The end convincingly relates to the body of the story. This may neatly tie up the loose ends or deliberately leave the reader guessing.

- The writer in control. Your child will have developed a point of view known as a 'narrative voice'. This takes the form of comments on the action, 'Now Sally should not have opened that door ...', or indications of characters' thoughts and feelings, 'Ben felt a chill of fear ...'.

Marking: 10 marks

Grammar

What you are looking for under this heading is the correct use of punctuation, capital letters, tenses and pronouns.

Styles

What you are looking for under this heading are sentence structure connectives and vocabulary.

Level 2

Look for:

- Sentences. At least two sentences where capital letters are used at the beginning and a full stop or question mark is used at the end.

Marking: 2 marks

Look for:

- Spoken language structures. Your child will write in much the same way as she/he would tell you the story.

- Connectives. Use of simple connectives to link ideas, 'and', and 'so', and 'then'.

- Vocabulary. The words your child uses will be very general: 'She had to get the bus' rather than 'She had to catch the bus'; 'Someone came into the room' rather than 'The old man came into the room'. Other examples of this general vocabulary include make, do, have, go, thing, something.

Marking: 2 marks

ENGLISH: Answers

Grammar (continued)   Styles (continued)

Level 3

Look for:

- Sentences. At least half the sentences on the first page should begin with a capital letter and end with a full stop or question mark.

Marking: 3 marks

Look for:

- Written language structures. Your child will begin to use sentences structures which are appropriate to written rather than spoken language.
- Connectives. These should be used to show contrast, 'but'; connection in time, 'when', 'also'; and explanation, 'so', 'because'.
- Vocabulary. Your child will be using vocabulary to give more detail, 'a blue book', 'one frosty morning', 'he ran quickly', 'she soon went to sleep'.

Marking: 3 marks

Level 4

Look for:

- Sentences. At least three-quarters of the sentences on the first page should begin with a capital letter and end with a full stop or question mark.
- Commas. Commas should be used to separate items on a list: 'The boy bought apples, pears, oranges and bananas'.
- Speech. If speech is included then speech marks should signal the beginning and ending of the spoken words in at least half of the instances.
- Question marks and exclamation marks. By this level, these should generally be used correctly.
- Tenses. Your child's writing should not wander from past to present tense or vice versa: 'Jim walked along the path. He runs across the road'.
- Pronouns. These should be consistent. Children often slip from the third person into the first person and back again, 'She was very happy. I had won the race and she got a prize'.

Marking: 4 marks

Look for:

- Written language structures. Your child should increasingly write in ways that do not rely on the way she/he would speak:

Spoken structure: 'They're really dreading going to the dentist.'

Written structure: 'The twins were not looking forward to their visit to the dentist.'

- Connectives. Using connectives to help order ideas and give emphasis, 'if', 'when', etc.
- Vocabulary. You will feel that your child's vocabulary has been chosen with some care to add detail and interest to the story, 'a large, dirty machine', 'a strong, howling wind'.

Marking: 4 marks

Level 5

Look for the following on the first page:

- Sentences. There should be no more than two mistakes in sentence punctuation.
- Commas. As well as for lists, commas should be used for parts of sentences, 'She rushed into the house, falling over the broken chair'.
- Speech. Speech marks and the comma to introduce/conclude direct speech should be correct in three-quarters of the instances used, 'I don't want to go,' he said. He said, 'I don't want to go.'
- Question marks and exclamation marks. These should be used correctly.

Marking: 5 marks

Look for:

- Written language structures. Your child will be using a variety of sentence constructions, 'He walked to the door ...', 'Walking to the door ...', 'As he walked to the door ...'.
- Connectives. Using connectives to refer back, 'I went to the shop that I had been to before ...' and to avoid repetition, 'The book was on the table and it was open at the first page ...'.
- Vocabulary. Your child will be using varied and appropriate vocabulary to give interest and detail to the story.

Marking: 5 marks

Letter writing

Purpose and organisation

What you are looking for under this heading are the form and content of the letter.

Level 2

Look for:
- Form. Your child will have a grasp of a simple letter format.
- Content. There will be some relevant points but they will not be developed or connected.
- Reader's knowledge. Your child will assume you know about the issues and not give full explanations or information.

Marking: 4 marks

Level 3

Look for:
- Form. A more secure grasp of the form of a letter.
- Content. There should be an introductory statement and some sensible connection between the points covered.
- Reader's knowledge. The letter will give more information and your child will have included details to add interest.

Marking: 6 marks

Level 4

Look for:
- Form. Most of the appropriate conventions of letter writing will be in place and your child should begin to separate the points by means of paragraphing.
- Content. There will be a relevant introduction, the main points clearly covered and the letter will end in a conclusive way, rather be left 'hanging in mid-air'.
- Reader's knowledge. The purpose of the letter will be clear and the information/background that the reader needs will, for the most part, be included.

Marking: 8 marks

Level 5

Look for:
- Form. The appropriate conventions of letter writing will be in place.
- Content. There will be good coverage of the main points linked by such phrases as, first of all, for instance, another problem.
- Reader's knowledge. Your child will have used the introduction to set out clearly the purpose of the letter and the conclusion to, sum up, appeal to the reader, suggest a course of action.

Marking: 10 marks

Grammar

What you are looking for under this heading is the correct use of punctuation, capital letters, tenses and pronouns.

Level 2

Look for:
- Sentences. At least two sentences where capital letters are used at the beginning and a full stop or question mark at the end.

Marking: 2 marks

Level 3

Look for:
- Sentences. At least half the sentences on the first page should begin with a capital letter and end with a full stop or question mark.

Marking: 3 marks

ENGLISH: Answers

Grammar (continued)

Level 4

Look for:
- Sentences. At least three-quarters of the sentences on the first page should begin with a capital letter and end with a full stop or question mark.
- Commas. Commas should be used to separate items on a list and in the address, greeting and signature.
- Question marks and exclamation marks. By this level, these should generally be used correctly.
- Tenses. Your child's writing should not wander from the past to present tense and vice versa, 'I was shocked at the state of your shop I am visiting yesterday'.
- Pronouns. These should be consistent. Children often slip from the third person into the first person and back again, 'She went in to the shop yesterday and I was not happy with what I saw'.

Marking: 4 marks

Level 5

Look for the following on the first page:
- Sentences. There should be no more than two mistakes in sentence punctuation.
- Commas. Commas should be used to separate parts of sentences, 'I am writing to you in the hope that you can, if at all possible, meet me ...'.
- Question marks and exclamation marks. These should be used correctly.

Marking: 5 marks

Styles

The levels of attainment under this heading for letter writing are the same as those for story writing. Refer to the Styles section of the marking criteria for Story Writing (see pages 29–30).

ENGLISH ANSWERS
Spelling and handwriting tests

Spelling

James was very **excited**. He had no idea **where** his parents were taking him on **holiday**. His mother said it was going to be a **surprise**. It had been **cloudy** when he had woken up but now the sun was shining.

Suddenly, he **remembered** that he hadn't packed his football so he rushed out of the **house** and into the shed. There it was, in the **corner**, almost hidden **under** a **pile** of old **newspapers**. As he **reached** down to pick it up there was a loud **bang**. The shed door had **blown** shut. There were no windows in the shed and he was in total **darkness**.

Gradually his eyes **adjusted** as there was **enough** light coming through a crack in the door for him to see a little. **Carefully** he **made** his way to the door, tripping over **dirty** rags and bits of **wood**. An **insect** brushed his face and he let out a loud **scream**. At last he felt the door **handle** but **neither** by **pushing** nor pulling could he get it open. He began to **rattle** the **knob** and shout loudly in the hope that **someone** would hear him.

30 marks

ENGLISH: Answers

Handwriting test

In order to get an idea of your child's level in handwriting you will need to decide which description and example best fits the sample of writing in the test. Award the number of marks shown for that level.

Level 2

Letters are not joined when writing.

> A resistor is to make things high and low power. Like if you cut a pencil in half and clip the wires on to the pencil then

Marking: 3 marks

Level 3

There is the beginning of clear, legible writing, showing the ability to join letters.

> The time machine whirred lights flashed across the transporter grid. They got brighter and brighter.

Marking: 4 marks

Level 4

The writing is more fluent and legible, showing the ability to join letters. Spaces between words will be regular, and the letters themselves of a similar size.

> The time machine whirred. Lights flashed across the transporter grid. They got brighter and brighter. The

Marking: 5 marks

Level 5

The writing is clear, legible and neat in a joined-up (cursive) style.

> The time machine whirred. Lights flashed across the transporter grid. They got brighter and brighter. The

Marking: 6 marks

ENGLISH ANSWERS
Finding a level for your child

The total number of marks a child could gain over the various elements of the English test are as follows:

Reading – (story)	40 marks
Reading – (information)	20 marks
Reading – (poetry)	15 marks
Writing (either story or letter)	20 marks
Spelling	30 marks
Handwriting	6 marks
Total	131 marks

One way of assessing your child's level is by adding the marks gained overall and using the table below:

Conversion of score into National Curriculum Levels

Level	Marks
Below Level 2	0 – 9
Level 2	10 – 33
Level 3	34 – 66
Level 4	67 – 98
Level 5	99 – 131

The table above is a somewhat simplistic indicator of level, as a child who did extremely well in, say, the reading test, but very badly in the spelling, could still gain an overall Level 4 mark whereas, in reality, the spelling in itself would have to improve for this to be reflected in the result of the overall national test.

A more sensible approach would be as follows:

If your child scores:

- up to a quarter of the marks for each individual test then grade the overall test as Level 2.
- between a quarter and a half of the marks for each individual test then grade the overall test as Level 3.
- between a half and three-quarters of the marks for each individual test then grade the overall test as Level 4.
- over three-quarters of the marks for each individual test then grade the overall test as Level 5.

MATHEMATICS
Testing your child's mathematics

What do the National Tests cover?

At Key Stage 2 your child will be studying four areas of mathematics in school. These are:

1. Using and Applying Mathematics
2. Number and Algebra
3. Shape, Space and Measures
4. Handling Data

The National Tests exclude Using and Applying Mathematics and concentrate on the other three areas: Number and Algebra; Shape, Space and Measures; Handling Data. Of these Number and Algebra is the most important and occupies the most space in the tests. For the tests in May your child will probably sit two papers. However, for ease and simplicity of marking we have presented the maths content in three papers which are explained below.

Setting the tests (time: 45 minutes each test)

1. The three tests need to be done in order. Test 1 covers Level 3, Test 2 covers Level 4 and Test 3 covers Level 5. Forty-five minutes should be allowed for each one.

2. Your child will need:
   - a pencil
   - a ruler
   - a calculator
   - tracing paper
   - a protractor

   It is suggested that you encourage your child just to cross out mistakes, rather than use a rubber.

3. Ensure that your child understands that they have to write answers on the blank lines. Sometimes boxes are provided which will ask your child to show how the answer has been worked out.

4. Explain the use of calculator symbols in the margin:

   means a calculator must be used.

   means a calculator may not be used.

   If no symbol appears, a calculator may be used if desired. However, from May 1996, pupils will not be allowed to use calculators in one of the test papers. It would therefore be helpful for your child not to make too much use of a calculator in these papers.

5. If your child gets stuck on any question, encourage them to go on to the next one.

6. Because these tests are graded for difficulty your child will find each test harder than the one before. Explain to children that they are unlikely to complete all the questions in all three tests and to do their best. If your child struggles on one particular test it is probably not worth proceeding to the next one but ensure that you offer praise for what has been achieved. You can get a good idea of your child's overall level in mathematics even if they cannot proceed beyond Test 1.

7. As with all the tests, ensure your child goes back over answers if they finish early.

MATHEMATICS
Test 1

1 Four children played a computer game and these are their scores:

| James | 146 | Alice | 251 |
| Hashim | 180 | Roy | 212 |

a. Who had the lowest score? _____

b. Who had the highest score? _____

c. Whose score is an odd number? _____

d. Whose score is in the 10 times table? _____

Dennis played the game later on and had a score of two hundred and three.

e. Write Dennis' score in numbers. _____

f. Which children did Dennis' score beat? _____

2

362   236
326   263

a. Write the numbers in order with the smallest first. _____

b. Write the highest number in words. _____

c. Two more numbers can be made using the digits 2 3 6.

   What are the other two numbers? _____ and _____

d. What is 362 to the nearest 10? _____

e. What is 263 to the nearest 100? _____

MATHEMATICS: Test 1

3 These are the temperatures in 5 cities on the 1st of January.

London 3°C   **Sydney 27°C**

Oslo −3°C

Moscow −10°C   **Los Angles 14°**

a. Which city was the hottest? _____

b. Which cities had temperatures below zero? _____
_____

c. Which city was the coldest? _____

4 This chart shows the number of children in the school with different eye colours.

	Hazel	Grey	Blue
Year 3	24	35	19
Year 4	30	26	14
Year 5	26	28	15
Year 6	28	32	12

a. How many children in Year 4 had grey eyes? _____

b. How many children in Year 6 had hazel eyes? _____

c. Which year group has 19 children with blue eyes? _____

d. How many children are there in Year 5? _____

e. How many children have hazel eyes? _____

5 Put a circle around the numbers which are in the 5 times table.

42   **12**

17   **30**

     25   **45**

10   **18**

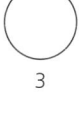

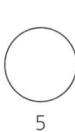

37

MATHEMATICS: Test 1

6 Danni adds 37 and 58 like this:
First she adds the units   7 + 8 = 15
Second she adds the tens   30 + 50 = 80
Then she adds them together 15 + 80 = 95

   a. Use Danni's method to add these two numbers: 26 and 49.

   Show your working.

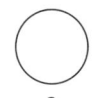

7 Some shapes have reflective symmetry. Put a tick (✔) in the column if the shape has reflective symmetry and a cross (✘) if it doesn't.

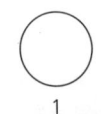

	Shape	✔ or ✘
a.		
b.		
c.		
d.		
e.		
f.		

8 Draw a shape of your own which has reflective symmetry.

TOTAL

MATHEMATICS: Test 1

9 Billy has used a calculator to help him with his sums. These are the sums which Billy did but the ⊞ button and the ⊠ button have been removed.
Put a ⊞ or ⊠ in the sums to make them correct.

a. 4 ☐ 3 ☐ 2 = 14

b. 5 ☐ 10 ☐ 6 = 56

c. 10 ☐ 3 ☐ 4 = 52

d. 3 ☐ 4 ☐ 5 = 60

10 Fill in the chart to show which of these shapes have curved faces and which have flat faces.

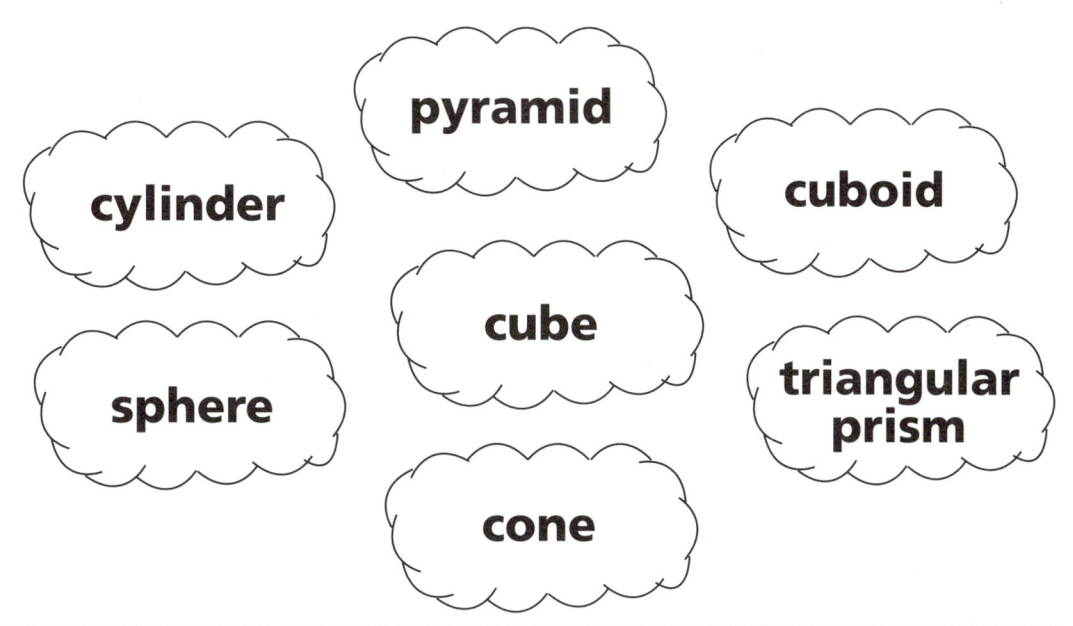

pyramid   cylinder   cuboid   cube   sphere   triangular prism   cone

with curved faces	with flat faces

11 On the left are three different items, and on the right are the units you would use to measure them, but they are mixed up. Match them up by drawing a line from the item on the left to the correct unit for measuring it on the right.

water in a bucket   grams

weight of a cake   centimetres

length of a pencil   litres

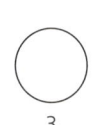

MATHEMATICS
Test 2

1. Football cards come in packs of 10. How many cards does each child buy?

Jane buys 6 packs _____ cards

Billy buys 14 packs _____ cards

Sandeep buys 27 packs _____ cards

Gareth buys 80 packs _____ cards

2. Fill in the numbers in the squares to make each sum correct:

a. 6 × ☐ = 54   b. ☐ × 8 = 56

c. 9 × ☐ = 63   d. 7 × ☐ = 42

3. Only one of these sums is correct. Tick (✔) the sum which is correct.

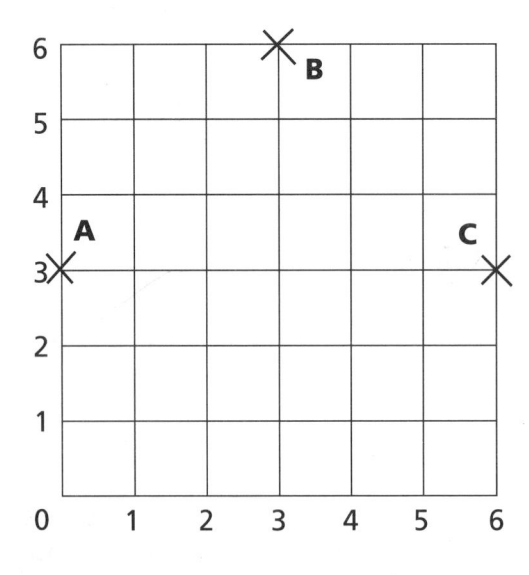

a. 27   b. 49   c. 36   d. 88
   × 6   × 8   × 7   × 9
   ---   ---   ---   ---
   142 ☐   384 ☐   242 ☐   792 ☐

4. A, B and C are three corners of a square.

a. What are the co-ordinates of

A _____

B _____

C _____

b. Put the fourth corner of the square on the grid and label it **D**.

c. Draw the square.

d. What is the area of the square? _____

MATHEMATICS: Test 2

5 $\boxed{4} \times \boxed{4} = 16$ and $\boxed{2} \times \boxed{2} = 4$

The same number in each sum is missing. Write down the number in these sums.

a. ☐ × ☐ = 25   **b.** ☐ × ☐ = 49

c. ☐ × ☐ = 100   **d.** ☐ × ☐ = 81

6 a. Only one of these shapes can be cut out and folded to make a cube. Which one? _____

A   B 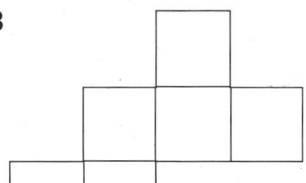   C

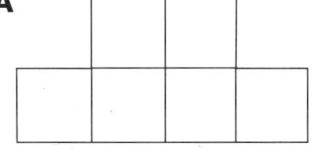

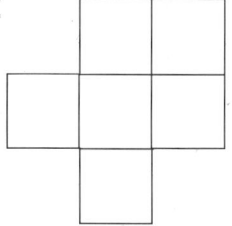

b. Which shape has the longest perimeter? _____

7 Use a mirror or tracing paper to complete these pictures.

a.

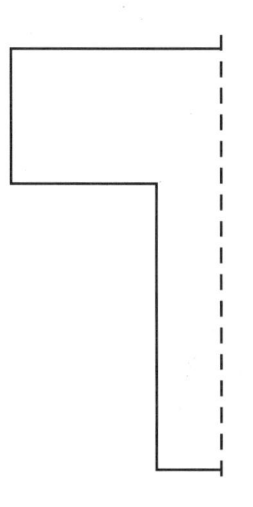

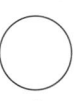

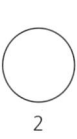

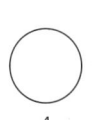

b.

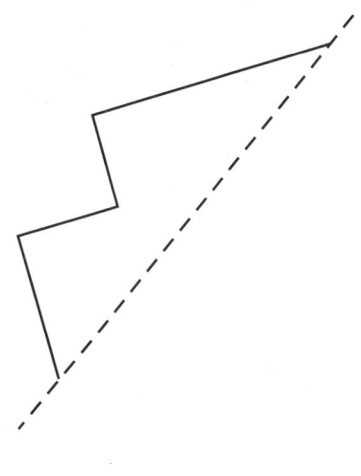

c.

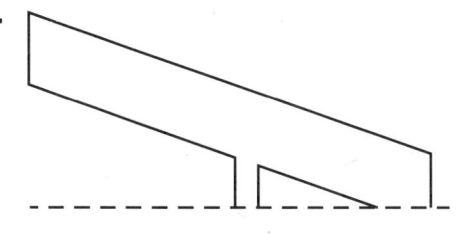

d.

4

2

4

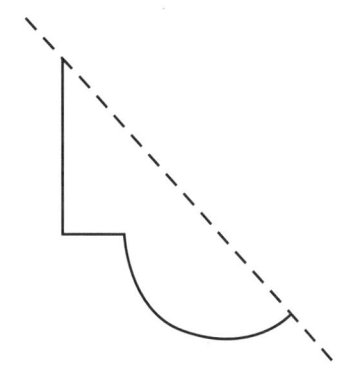

TOTAL

10

MATHEMATICS: Test 2

8 Andy has collected 80 stamps.

    a. 50% are from Britain: how many is that? _____

    b. 25% are from the USA: how many is that? _____

    c. 10% are from France: how many is that? _____

    d. 75% are rectangle shape: how many is that? _____

9 Four children estimate the length of the school mini-bus.

Put a tick in the box by the most sensible estimate

    Patrick – 40 cm ☐   **Ann – 4 metres** ☐

    Don – 140 cm ☐   **Sue – 40 metres** ☐

10 The school netball team played 20 games in a season and these are the number of goals scored.

number of games	number of goals
1	0
0	1
5	2
6	3
8	4

a. Draw a bar line graph to show the information.

    b. How many goals were scored in the season?

    _____

    c. What was the mean number of goals scored?

    _____

TOTAL

13

MATHEMATICS: Test 2

11 a. 15 000 is the same as how many hundreds? _____

b. 2000 is the same as how many tens? _____

c. How many pounds are the same as 120 ten pences? _____

d. Drawing pins are packed in boxes of 100. How many boxes would be needed to pack 40 000 drawing pins? _____

12 How are these number machines changing the numbers going IN to the numbers coming OUT?

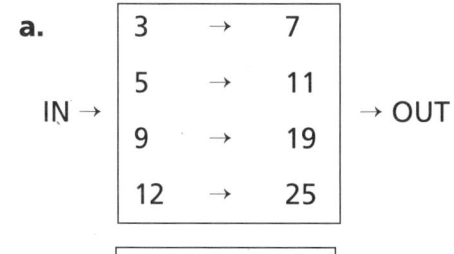

a. IN → | 3 → 7 / 5 → 11 / 9 → 19 / 12 → 25 | → OUT

answer [ ]

b. IN → | 3 → 3 / 9 → 5 / 15 → 7 / 30 → 12 | → OUT

answer [ ]

13 Work out the volume of each box.

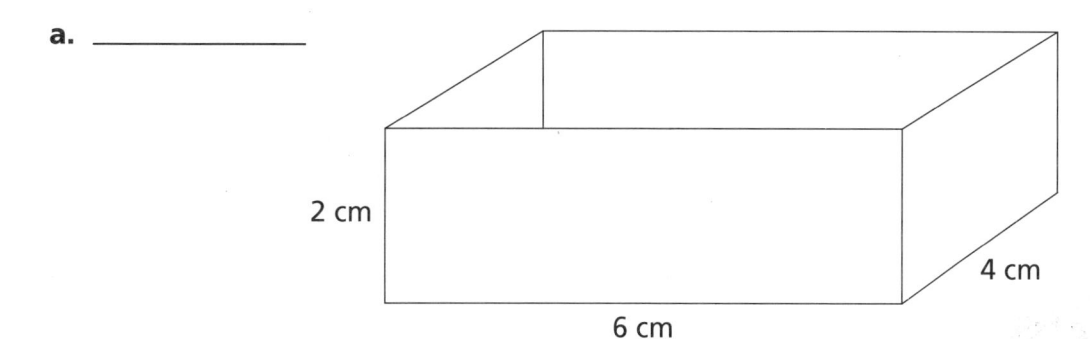

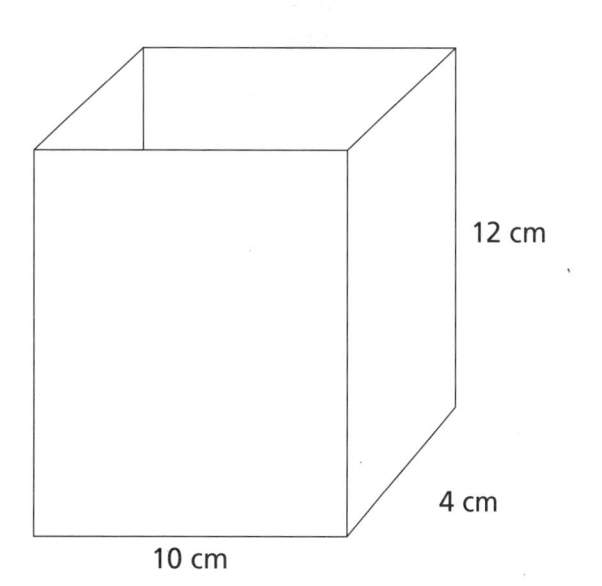

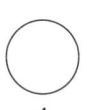

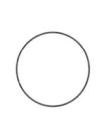

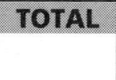

a. _____

2 cm
6 cm
4 cm

b. _____

12 cm
10 cm
4 cm

MATHEMATICS: Test 2

14 This tally chart shows how many house points are collected in one week.

Chichester	ʖʖʖ ʖʖʖ ʖʖʖ ǁ
Drake	ʖʖʖ ʖʖʖ ǁǁǁǁ
Murray	ʖʖʖ ʖʖʖ ʖʖʖ ʖʖʖ ʖʖʖ ǁǁǁ
Nelson	ʖʖʖ ʖʖʖ ʖʖʖ ʖʖʖ

a. How many points did each house gain?

Chichester _____   Drake _____

Murray _____   Nelson _____

b. Complete this simple line graph to show the number of house points gained by each team. (Chichester has been done for you.)

15 What is the median and mode in each row?

a. 2, 1, 3, 4, 2, 1, 3, 2, 2   mode _____ median _____

b. 10, 5, 15, 5, 5, 10, 10, 15, 5   mode _____ median _____

c. 1, 0, 1, 1, 1, 0, 1, 0   mode _____ median _____

MATHEMATICS
Test 3

1 These items cost this much:

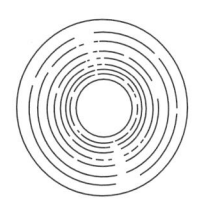

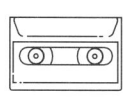

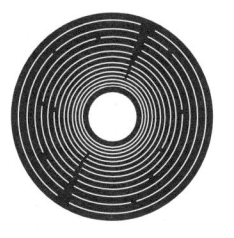

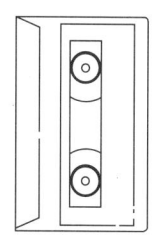

CDs
£12.50

cassettes
£8.09

records
£2.35

video
£10.40

Work out the cost of

a. Ten CDs _____

b. One hundred cassettes _____

c. One hundred records _____

d. One thousand videos _____

2 A builder lays four paths of these lengths:

A 4.62 m   **B** 10.85 m   **C** 7.30 m   **D** 8.07 m

He then adds an extra 2.68 m on to each path.
Now how long will each path be?

A _____   **B** _____   **C** _____   **D** _____

3 **a.** Which is the larger out of 'one-third of 27' or '20% of 50' and by how much?

_____

b. Which is smaller out of 'one-fifth of 400' or '75% of 80' and by how much?

_____

MATHEMATICS: Test 3

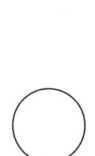

4 Help the teacher by marking these sums for her. Put a tick (✔) if they are right and a (✗) if they are wrong.

a.   267
   ×   14
   ────
  1068
 +2670
 ────
 3638 ☐

b.   419
   ×   27
   ────
  2933
 + 838
 ────
 3771 ☐

c.   342
   ×   36
   ────
 20520
 +10260
 ─────
 30780 ☐

5 a. A child thinks that 3.9 × 3.9 is closer to 14 than 17. Is she correct?

_____

b. Explain how you made a decision about part **a**. _____

_____

_____

6 Join up the measurements on the left with a sensible estimate on the right.

                                                         3 km

Length of a finger   400g

                                                      3 mm

Weight of a can of coke   200 ml

                                                      10 l

Length of an ant   6 m

                                                      4 kg

Capacity of a fire bucket   6 cm

                                                      2 l

MATHEMATICS: Test 3

7 **a.** In box **A**, draw a quadrilateral which has no lines of symmetry.

b. In box **B**, draw a quadrilateral which has four lines of symmetry.

A.

B.

c. In box **C**, draw a quadrilateral which has rotational symmetry.

d. In box **D**, draw a triangle which has rotational symmetry order 3.

C.

D.

8 Write down the name of a quadrilateral which has no lines of symmetry and rotational symmetry order 2.

9 Name a shape with rotational symmetry order 8.

MATHEMATICS: Test 3

10 This pie chart shows the colours of teachers' cars in the car park at Horndean Junior School.

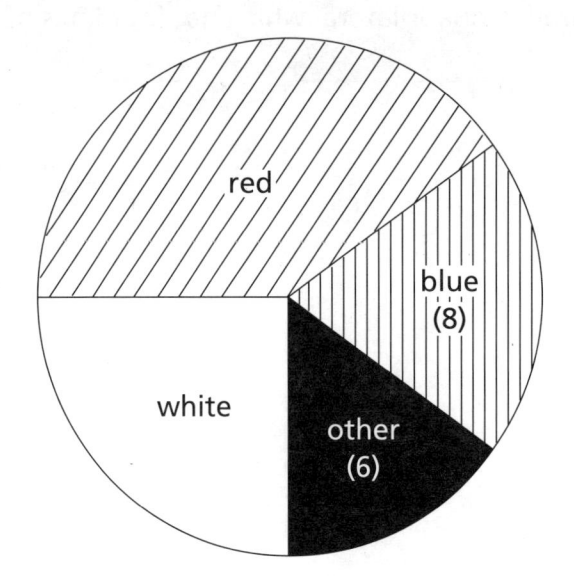

There are 40 cars in the car park.

   a. 25% of the cars are white. How many is that? _____

   b. What percentage of the cars are red? _____

   c. What fraction of the cars are blue? _____

   d. What percentage of the cars are not blue? _____

11 Work out the mean of each row of numbers.

   a. 3, 8, 16   _____

   b. 10, 40, 70, 80   _____

   c. 5p, 10p, 20p, 50p, £1.00   _____

   d. 24, 35, 18, 92, 47, 26, 54, 40   _____

12 A 10p is thrown in the air three times and comes down heads each time. What is the probability it will come down heads on the fourth throw? Explain your answer.

_____

_____

MATHEMATICS: Test 3

13 Write each of these fractions as a percentage.

a. $\frac{1}{2}$ = _____ % b. $\frac{1}{4}$ = _____ % c. $\frac{3}{4}$ = _____ %

d. $\frac{1}{10}$ = _____ % e. $\frac{2}{5}$ = _____ %

14 Complete each sequence of numbers by putting the correct number in each square.

a. 3   6   ☐   24   48   ☐

b. 1   4   ☐   ☐   ☐   36

c. 40   20   10   ☐   ☐   ☐

d. 1000   100   ☐   1   ☐

15 One of these shapes has an area of 10 cm² and a perimeter of 15 cm. Which one?

a. 4 cm, $3\frac{1}{2}$ cm

b. 2 cm, 5 cm

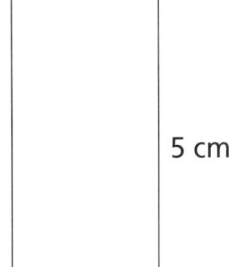

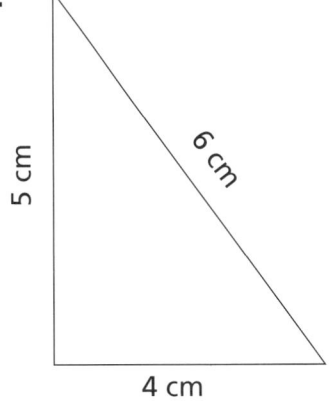

c. 5 cm, 6 cm, 4 cm

Answer _____

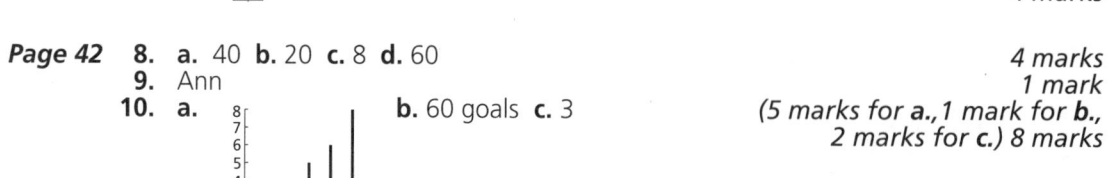

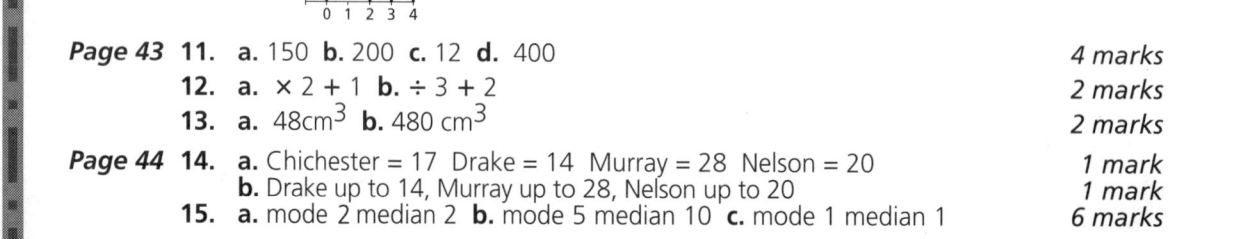

MATHEMATICS
Answers

Some questions do not have a simple right or wrong answer and in these cases you will have to use your discretion in awarding marks. A conversion chart is provided for each test (test 2 and test 3 have the same mark scheme). Because each test is more difficult than the previous one simply study your child's performance against the last test they sat in order to get an impression of their level in mathematics.

Test 1

Page 36
1. **a.** James **b.** Alice **c.** Alice **d.** Hashim **e.** 203 **f.** James and Hashim — *6 marks*
2. **a.** 236, 263, 326, 362
   b. Three hundred and sixty two
   c. 623 and 632 **d.** 360 **e.** 300 — *5 marks*

Page 37
3. **a.** Sydney **b.** Oslo and Moscow **c.** Moscow — *3 marks*
4. **a.** 26 **b.** 28 **c.** Year 3 **d.** 69 **e.** 108 — *5 marks*
5. 10, 25, 30, 45 only — *(one extra mark for not marking any other numbers) 5 marks*

Page 38
6. **a.** 6 + 9 = 15, 20 + 40 = 60, 60 + 15 = 75 — *3 marks*
7. **a.** ✔ **b.** ✘ **c.** ✔ **d.** ✔ **e.** ✘ **f.** ✔ — *2 marks*
8. Various shapes may be drawn. — *1 mark*

Page 39
9. **a.** ×+ **b.** ×+ **c.** +× **d.** ×× — *4 marks*
10. curved faces – sphere, cylinder, cone;
    flat faces – prism, cuboid, pyramid, cone, cube, cylinder — *9 marks*
11. water – litres; weight – grams; length – centimetres — *3 marks*

Test 2

Page 40
1. Jane – 60, Billy – 140, Sandeep – 270, Gareth – 800 — *4 marks*
2. **a.** 9 **b.** 7 **c.** 7 **d.** 6 — *4 marks*
3. d is correct — *2 marks*
4. **a.** A (0, 3), B (3, 6), C(6, 3) **b.** (3, 0) **d.** 18cm^2 — *4 marks*

Page 41
5. **a.** 5 **b.** 7 **c.** 10 **d.** 9 — *4 marks*
6. **a.** B **b.** B — *2 marks*
7. **a.** **b.** **c.** **d.** — *4 marks*

Page 42
8. **a.** 40 **b.** 20 **c.** 8 **d.** 60 — *4 marks*
9. Ann — *1 mark*
10. **a.** **b.** 60 goals **c.** 3 — *(5 marks for **a.**, 1 mark for **b.**, 2 marks for **c.**) 8 marks*

Page 43
11. **a.** 150 **b.** 200 **c.** 12 **d.** 400 — *4 marks*
12. **a.** × 2 + 1 **b.** ÷ 3 + 2 — *2 marks*
13. **a.** 48cm^3 **b.** 480 cm^3 — *2 marks*

Page 44
14. **a.** Chichester = 17 Drake = 14 Murray = 28 Nelson = 20 — *1 mark*
    b. Drake up to 14, Murray up to 28, Nelson up to 20 — *1 mark*
15. **a.** mode 2 median 2 **b.** mode 5 median 10 **c.** mode 1 median 1 — *6 marks*

MATHEMATICS: Answers

Test 3

Page 45
1. a. £125.00 b. £809.00 c. £235.00
   d. £10 400   *4 marks*
2. A = 7.30 B = 13.53 C = 9.98
   D = 10.75   *4 marks*
3. 20% of 50 by 1 b. 75% of 80 by 20   *2 marks*

Page 46
4. a. × b. × c. ×   *6 marks*
5. a. Yes
   b. To the effect that 3.9 is just under 4 and 4 × 4 is 16,
      so the answer cannot be more than 16.
              (1 mark for correct answer, 1 mark for explanation) 2 marks
6. a. finger – 6 cm, coke – 400 g, ant – 3 mm, bucket – 10 l   *4 marks*

Page 47
7. a. Answers can vary b. square
   c. rectangle, square and others
   d. equilateral triangle   *8 marks*
8. parallelogram   *1 mark*
9. octagon   *1 mark*

Page 48
10. a. 10 b 40% c. $\frac{8}{10}$, $\frac{4}{40}$, $\frac{2}{10}$, $\frac{1}{5}$ d. 80%   *4 marks*
11. a. 9 b 50 c. 37p d. 42   *4 marks*
12. 1 in 2, $\frac{1}{2}$ or 50% are acceptable. Previous throws do not affect the next one.
              (1 mark for correct answer, 2 marks for explanation) 3 marks

Page 49
13. a. 50 b. 25 c. 75 d. 10 e. 40   *5 marks*
14. a. 12, 96 b. 9, 16, 25 c. 5, 2$\frac{1}{2}$, 1$\frac{1}{4}$ d. 10, $\frac{1}{10}$ (0.1)   *4 marks*
15. c.   *1 mark*

Conversion of score into National Curriculum Levels

Test 1 (Level 3)

Level 2 or below	0 – 10
Some work towards Level 3 with many areas to be addressed	11 – 20
Working within Level 2 and towards Level 3	21 – 33
Working well at Level 3	34 – 46

Test 2 (Level 4) and/or Test 3 (Level 5)

Working below level tested	0 – 15
Some work towards level tested with many areas to be addressed	16 – 27
Working within prior level and towards the level tested	28 – 43
Working well at level tested	44 – 53

SCIENCE
Testing your child's science

What do the National Tests cover?

At Key Stage 2 your child will be studying four areas of science in school. These are:
1. Experimental and Investigative Science
2. Life Processes and Living Things
3. Materials and their Properties
4. Physical Processes

The National Tests exclude Experimental and Investigative Science, which usually consists of practical work, and concentrate on science knowledge, which is covered by the other three areas. For the tests in May your child will probably sit two papers; however for ease and simplicity we have provided coverage of the science content in one paper which follows their format.

Setting the test (time: 30 minutes)
1. Ensure that your child understands where to write the answers in the spaces provided. Explain that some questions will ask for the answer to be drawn rather than written. It is important that answers are drawn as clearly as possible.
2. The test uses some scientific vocabulary (e.g. organ, transparent). If your child has difficulty reading some of these words you may read them out, however you should not explain their meaning. Some answers will require a similar use of a specific scientific word (e.g. condensation) to get a mark. The use of correct scientific language is an important feature from Level 4 on.
3. Allow 30 minutes for the test.

SCIENCE
Test

1 | Living things

Terrier   Grass snake   Cockatoo   Guppy   Daisy

Which **three** things do all the living things here do?

Tick ✔

swim ☐   jump ☐   grow ☐

feed ☐   fly ☐   reproduce ☐

3

2 | Ourselves

Write down two ways in which you keep your teeth and gums healthy.

_____

_____

2

3 | Ourselves

Name these organs.

A. _____

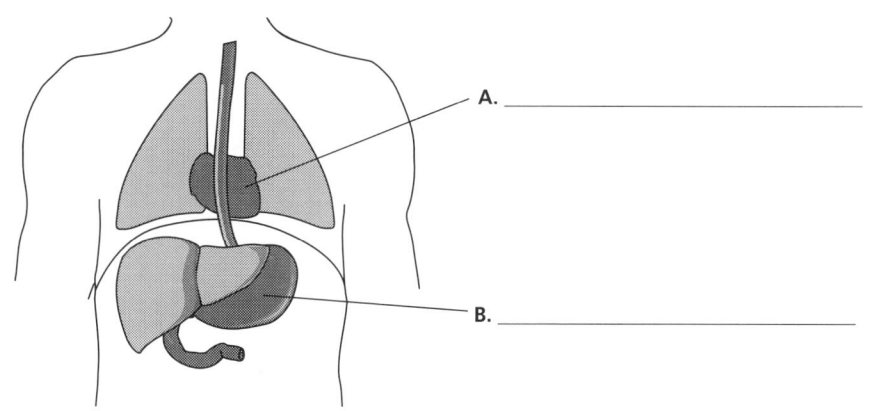

B. _____

2

TOTAL

7

4. Using materials

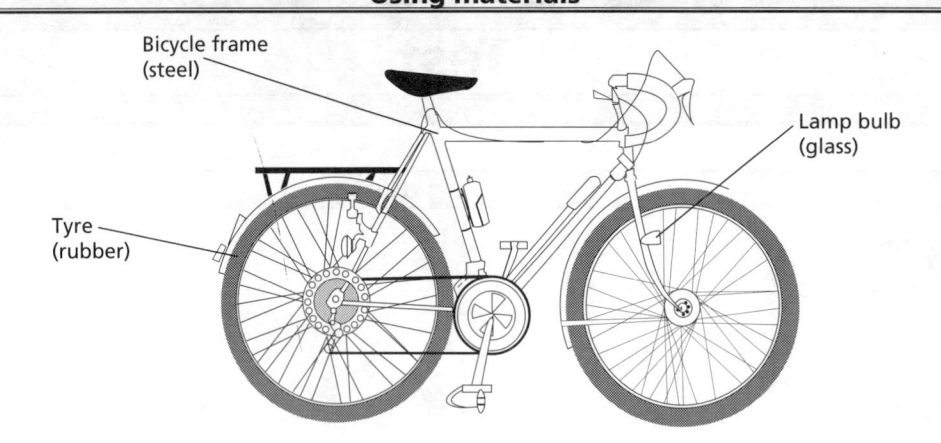

Bicycle frame (steel)
Lamp bulb (glass)
Tyre (rubber)

Tick ✔ one box to show why these materials are used.

A. Bicycle frame is made from steel because it is

cold ☐   strong ☐   shiny ☐

B. Lamp bulb is made from glass because it is

hard ☐   transparent ☐   sharp ☐

C. Tyre is made from rubber because it is

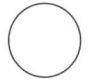

round ☐   black ☐   stretchy ☐

5. Light

A torch is switched on in a dark room.

A. Draw the shadow of the vase on the wall in the picture.

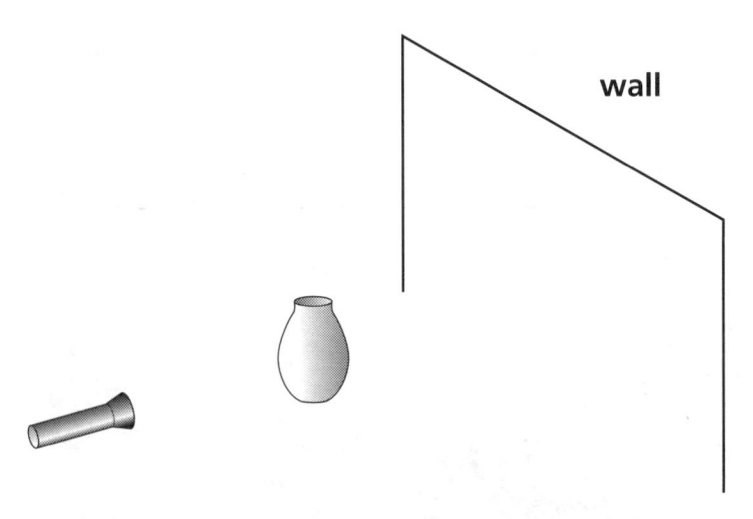

wall

B. Why does the vase cast a shadow?

_____

_____

_____

6 Magnetism

Which of these things will a magnet attract? Tick ✔ the correct boxes.

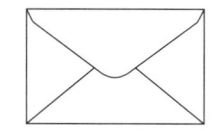

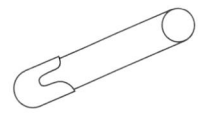

steel pin ☐   envelope ☐   solid gold ring ☐   safety pin ☐

Magnets attract magnetic materials. Write in the name of a magnetic material.

_____

7 Plant life

The Smith family are on holiday for three weeks. Their pot plants are indoors with the curtains drawn.

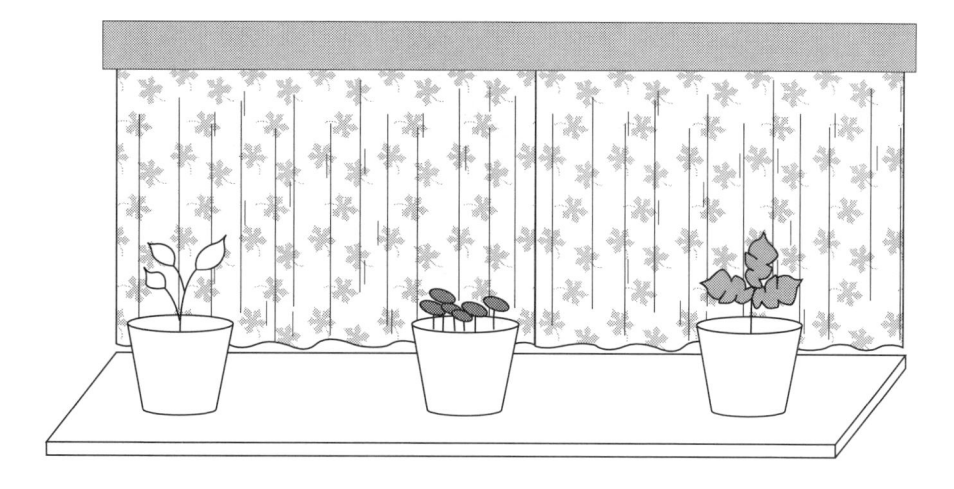

Write in two reasons why the plants may not be growing well when the family come home.

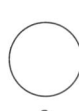

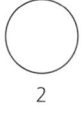

_____

_____

_____

_____

_____

SCIENCE: Test

8. Plant life cycle

| stigma | petals | female | stamen |

These words have been left out of the sentences below. Write the words where they go. Use each word only once.

Insects are attracted to the flowers by their _____. Pollen is made by the _____. The pollen is carried to another flower of the same kind, where it lands on the _____. This is a _____ part of the flower.

9. Electricity

Finish the drawings so that the lamp comes on in all three models.

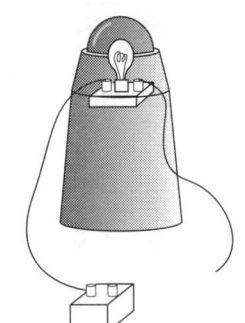

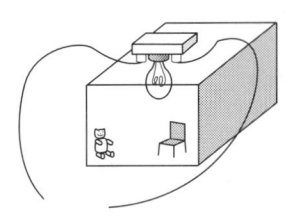

10. Forces

For each toy draw in the direction of the force that makes it move.

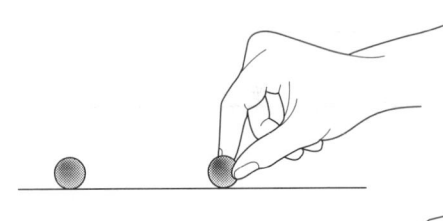

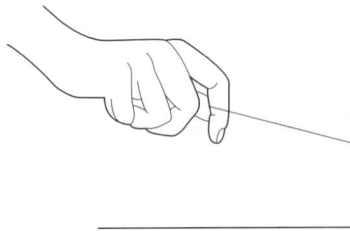

SCIENCE: Test

11 **Classifying animals**

Tom found some small animals.

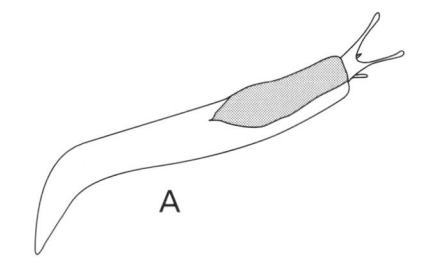

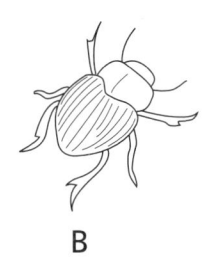

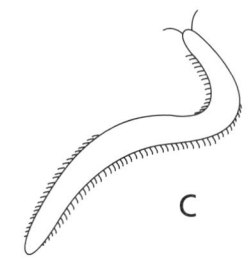

A   B   C

He made a key to name them. Use the key and write in the animals' names below.

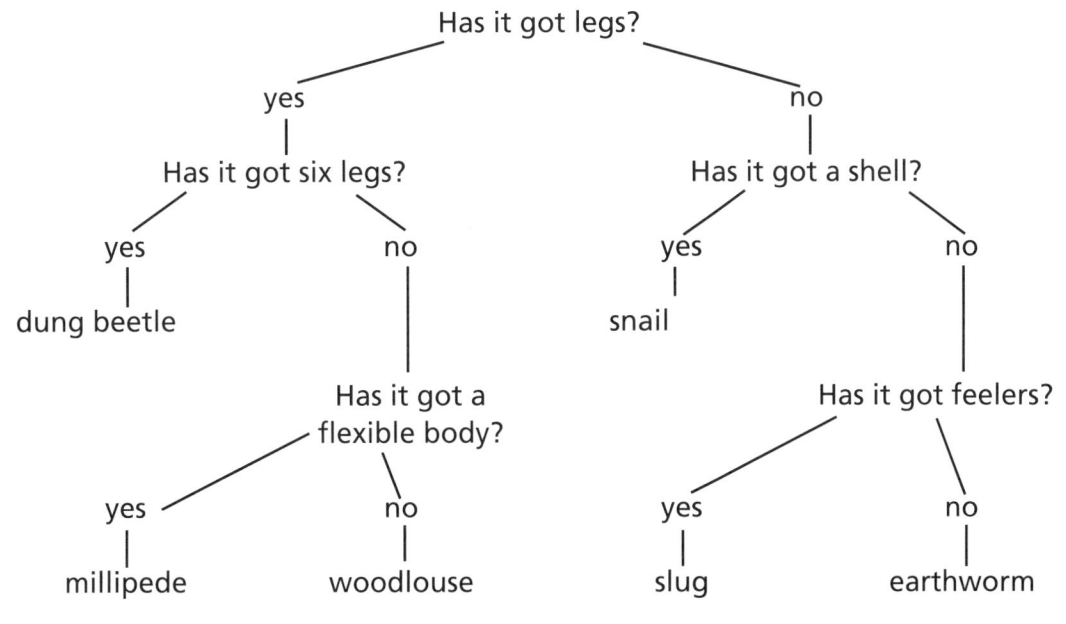

```
                    Has it got legs?
                   /               \
                 yes                no
                  |                  |
          Has it got six legs?   Has it got a shell?
           /         \            /          \
         yes          no        yes           no
          |            |          |            |
     dung beetle       |        snail          |
                Has it got a              Has it got feelers?
                flexible body?             /          \
                 /        \              yes           no
               yes         no             |             |
                |           |            slug        earthworm
             millipede  woodlouse
```

Name the animals

A _____

B _____

C _____

SCIENCE: Test

12 | Changing materials

A raw egg goes hard when boiled in water.
We cannot change a hard-boiled egg back into a raw one.

Which of these can we change back?

Tick ✔ yes *or* no.

A Cake mix

Cake mix → oven → cakes

Can we change the cakes back?

yes ☐   no ☐

B Candle wax

Candle wax → melted wax

Can we change the wax back?

yes ☐   no ☐

C Nail

iron nail in water → rusty nail

Can we change the nail back?

yes ☐   no ☐

D Ice

ice → water

Can we change the water back?

yes ☐   no ☐

13 | Separating mixtures

If salt water was left untouched in a shallow dish, on a window sill, for several weeks, what would you expect to happen?

_____

_____

_____

_____

14 Properties of materials

Metals are very useful because of their properties. Say why the metals are used in these ways:

Aluminium is used in making saucepans because _____

_____

Copper is used in making electrical wiring because _____

_____

15 Forces

Why do some racing cyclists have helmets shaped like this?

_____

_____

16 The Earth in space

The Earth moves around the Sun. How long does the Earth take to orbit the Sun once?

_____

This diagram shows the Earth and the Moon. **Draw** in the path taken by the Moon as it moves.

(Not drawn to scale)

SCIENCE: Test

17 | **Sound**

To get a sound out of chime bars, we tap them.

Tick ✔ the word that describes what happens to the bar when we tap it.

rotates ☐   vibrates ☐   bangs ☐

18 | **Forces**

A metal spring is fixed at one end to a clamp stand. What measurements would you need to find out what happens to the spring when three different weights are hung on the spring in turn?

_____
_____
_____
_____

19 | **Animals in their environment**

A Write in the names of these living things as a food chain.

Blue-tit   Red Admiral caterpillar   Sparrowhawk   Stinging nettle

☐ → ☐ → ☐ → ☐

B Name the food producer _____

SCIENCE: Test

20 | Humans

Complete these sentences.

The main function of the heart is to _____

_____

The main function of the lungs is to _____

_____

21 | Classifying materials

Which of these are solid, which are liquid, which are gas?

Write in   ⬜ s for solid
           ⬜ l for liquid
           ⬜ g for gas

A jelly ☐   **B** tomato sauce ☐   **C** ice lolly ☐   **D** biscuit ☐   **E** air ☐   **F** cooking oil ☐

Complete these sentences. Write in ⬜ s for solids ⬜ l for liquids ⬜ g for gases

G ☐ have a fixed shape

H ☐ can be easily squashed

I ☐ and ☐ take the shape of any container they are put in.

22 | Changing materials

Which word describes what happens to the water if it is left to boil in a kettle?

filtrates ☐

melts ☐

evaporates ☐

What may happen on the window in the same room as the boiling kettle?

_____

_____

SCIENCE: Test

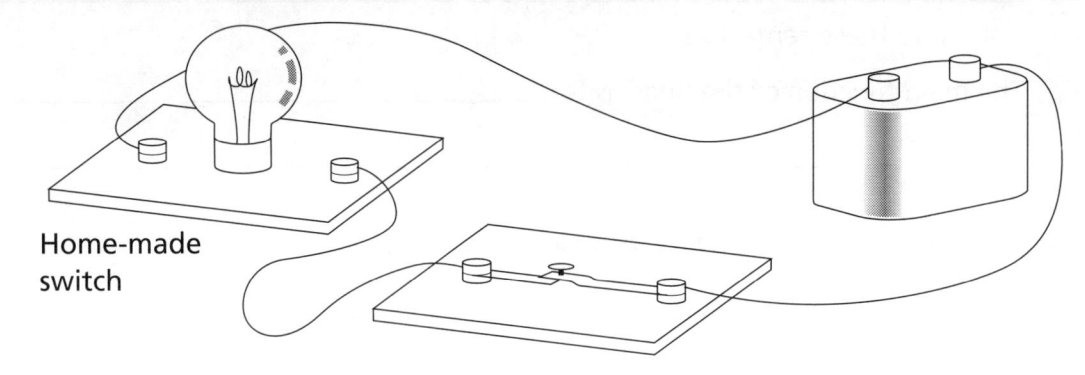

23 | **Electricity**

Home-made switch

Draw a circuit diagram to show the circuit above.

Now draw a circuit diagram with a battery and two lamps in series in it.

SCIENCE
Answers

1 feed/grow/reproduce 3 marks
Give no marks if more than three ticked.

2 clean teeth regularly/once or twice a day/after meals *and/or* avoid sugary goods and drinks *and/or* visit the dentist regularly *Give maximum 2 marks*

3 A. heart B. stomach 2 marks

4 A. strong B. transparent C. stretchy 3 marks

5 A. Shadow of vase should be similar in shape to vase, any size and shaded. 1 mark
Give no mark if not shaped like vase or not shaded.

B. Shadow cast because light cannot pass through the vase. 1 mark

6 steel pin and safety pin 2 marks
Give one mark if only one of these is ticked, and none if more than these two ticked.

7 not enough light/sun *and/or* not enough/no water *and/or* not warm enough 2 marks
Give maximum two marks. Ignore other answers (for example, not enough attention).

8 petals, stamen, stigma, female 2 marks
Give 1 mark if two words are in correct places.

9 The drawings should look like this: 3 marks

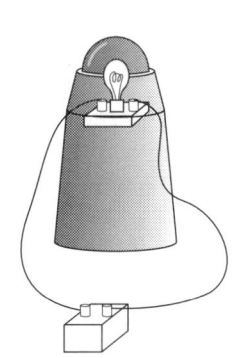

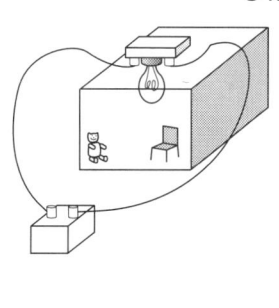

Make sure the wires are drawn to look unbroken from lamp to and from battery.

10 The direction of the arrows is as shown here: 3 marks

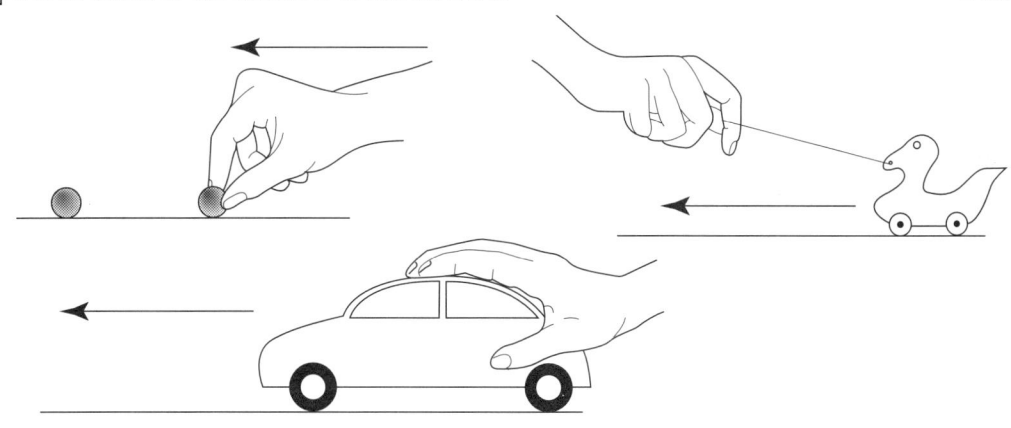

11 A. slug B. dung beetle C. millipede 3 marks

12 A. no B. yes C. no D. yes 4 marks

13 The water would evaporate into the air *and* salt/salt crystals would be left on the dish. 2 marks

SCIENCE: Test

14 A. good conductor of heat *or* light in weight *or* does not corrode easily *1 mark*
B. good conductor of electricity *1 mark*

15 The shape reduces air resistance and the cyclist can therefore go faster. *1 mark*

16 365 $\frac{1}{4}$ days *or* 365 days *or* one year *1 mark*
The path of the moon can be drawn like this: *1 mark*

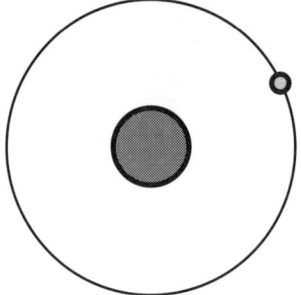

17 vibrates *1 mark*

18 The length of the spring without 'weight' hung from it and the lengths of the spring when each of the three 'weights' is hung from it *2 marks*

19 A. stinging nettle → Red admiral → Blue-tit → Sparrowhawk *1 mark*
B. Stinging nettle *1 mark*

20 The heart pumps blood around the body *or* The heart pumps blood to provide oxygen for the body *or* The heart pumps blood to the lungs to get oxygen from the air. *1 mark*
The lungs draw air into the body so that it may get oxygen *or* Keep the body supplied with oxygen *or* Allow gas exchange *1 mark*
   Give no mark for other answers (For example, it beats, or allows us to love).
   Give no mark for 'breathe' unless oxygen or gas exchange is also mentioned.

21 A. s B. l C. s D. s E. g F. l *3 marks*
   Give 1 mark for every two correct answers.
G. s H. g I. l and g *2 marks*
   Give 2 marks if all three correct. Give 1 mark if one or two correct.

22 Evaporates *1 mark*
The windows may get condensation on them/the water vapour may condense on the windows. *1 mark*
   Only give the mark if the word 'condense' or 'condensation' is used.

23 The circuits should look like this:
A. *1 mark*   B. *1 mark*

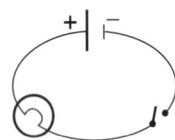

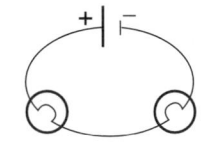

Conversion of score into National Curriculum Levels

Your child has not had enough experience in Science. Wait until they have more experience then try the test again.	0 – 10
Working towards Level 3	11 – 17
Working at Level 3	18 – 24
Working towards Level 4	25 – 35
Working at Level 4	36 – 42
Working towards Level 5	43 – 47
Working at least at Level 5. Your child may have reached Level 6 but this cannot be confirmed using this test.	48 – 54